really easy piano

ELTON JOHN

Bennie and the Jets	4
Blue Eyes	3
Can You Feel the Love Tonight	6
Candle in the Wind	8
Crocodile Rock	10
Daniel	48
Don't go Breaking my Heart	12
Don't Let the Sun Go Down on Me	14
Electricity	16
Goodbye Yellow Brick Road	18
I Guess That's Why They Call it the Blues	20
I Want Love	22
I'm Still Standing	24
NikIta	26
The One	28
Passengers	30
Rocket Man	32
Sacrifice	34
Sad Songs (Say so Much)	36
Saturday Night's Alright for Fighting	38
Something About the Way You Look Tonight	40
Sorry Seems to Be the Hardest Word	42
Tiny Dancer	44
Your Song	46

ISBN: 978-1-84609-784-3

For all works contained herein:
Unauthorized copying, arranging, adapting, recording, Internet posting, public performance,
or other distribution of the music in this publication is an infringement of copyright.
Infringers are liable under the law.

Visit Hal Leonard Online at
www.halleonard.com

Contact us:
Hal Leonard
7777 West Bluemound Road
Milwaukee, WI 53213
Email: info@halleonard.com

In Europe, contact:
Hal Leonard Europe Limited
42 Wigmore Street
Marylebone, London, W1U 2RY
Email: info@halleonardeurope.com

In Australia, contact:
Hal Leonard Australia Pty. Ltd.
4 Lentara Court
Cheltenham, Victoria, 3192 Australia
Email: info@halleonard.com.au

Blue Eyes

JUMP UP!

Words & Music by Elton John & Gary Osborne

The album from which this song was taken also featured the song *Empty Garden (Hey Hey Johnny)*, a tribute to John Lennon. However, whilst *Blue Eyes* reached No. 8 on the UK Charts, *Empty Garden* failed to break the Top 50.

Hints & Tips: Practise the right hand descending scale in thirds (bars 12–13) very slowly keeping your fingers curved and close to the keys as they cross over one another.

© Copyright 1982 Big Pig Music Limited.
Universal Music Publishing Limited.
All rights in Germany administered by Universal Music Publ. GmbH.
All Rights Reserved. International Copyright Secured.

GOODBYE YELLOW BRICK ROAD

Bennie And The Jets

Words & Music by Elton John & Bernie Taupin

This song tells the story of Bennie and the Jets, a fictional band of whom Elton is a supposed fan; the lyrics portraying the greed and glitz of the music industry in the 1970s. Despite the dark aspect to the song, and Elton's reluctance to release it as a single, it topped the US Charts in 1973.

Hints & Tips: Make sure you keep the introduction (bars 1–4) very steady, however boring it may seem! If you rush them you'll struggle when you reach the semiquavers and the slightly tricky fingering further into the song.

© Copyright 1973 Dick James Music Limited.
Universal/Dick James Music Limited.
All rights in Germany administered by Universal Music Publ. GmbH.
All Rights Reserved. International Copyright Secured.

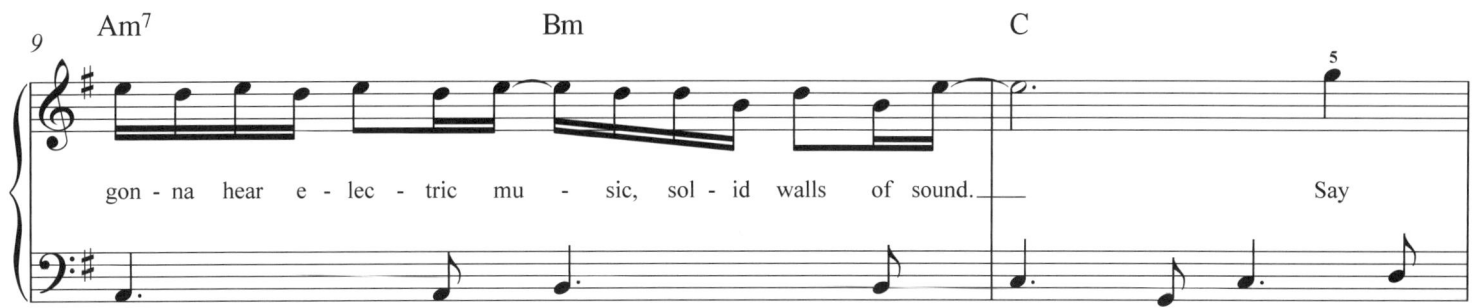
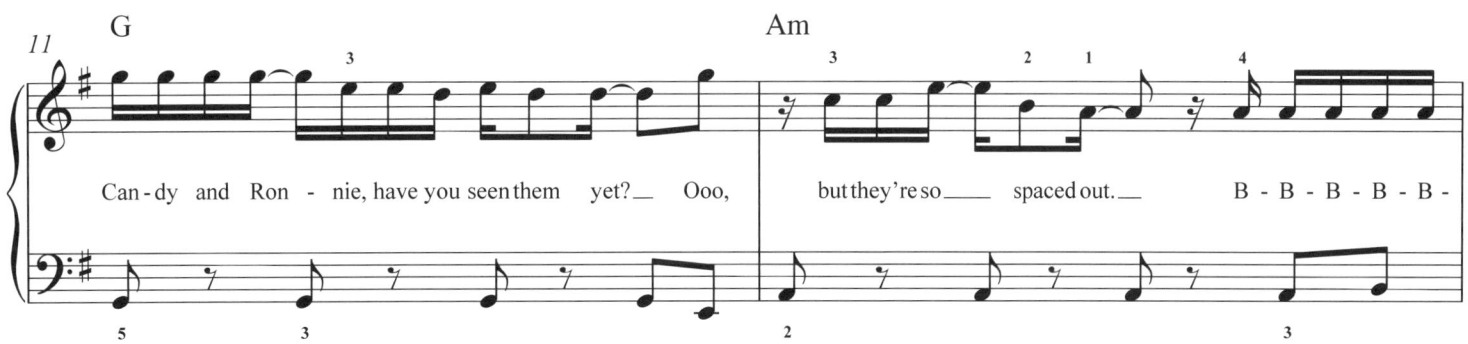

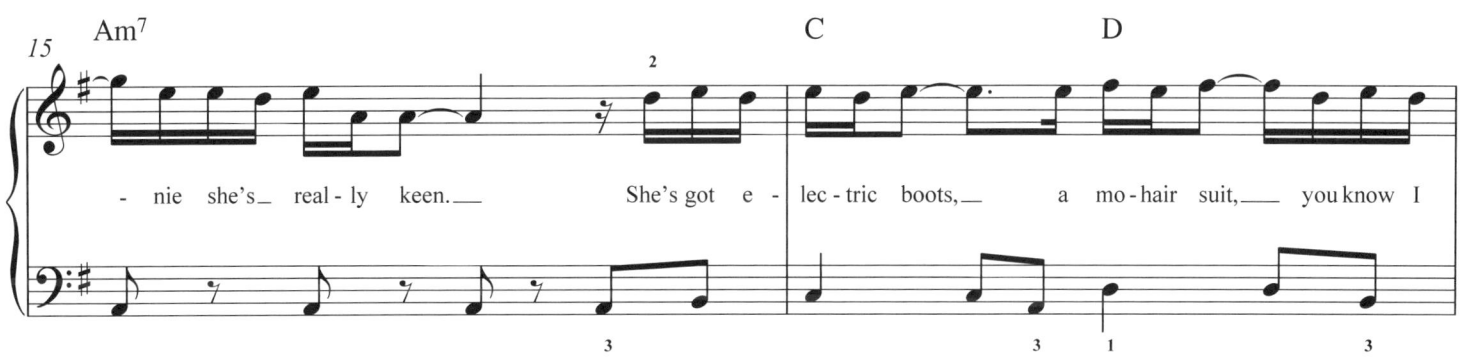
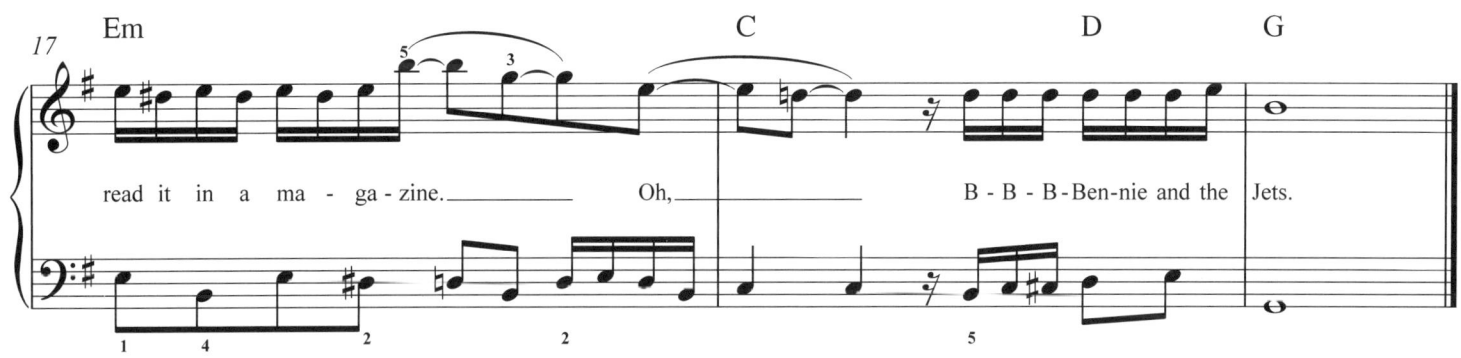

FROM 'THE LION KING'
Can You Feel The Love Tonight
Words by Tim Rice. Music by Elton John

This award-winning song was written for Disney's animated film *The Lion King*. It won the 1994 Academy and Golden Globe Awards for Best Original Song. It also earned Elton a Grammy for Best Male Pop Vocal Performance.

Hints & Tips: Most of the rhythms and fingerings in this piece are straightforward so take the opportunity to be expressive in your performance by thinking about phrasing (where to 'breathe') and dynamics (loud and quiet).

© Copyright 1994 Wonderland Music Company Incorporated, USA.
All Rights Reserved. International Copyright Secured.

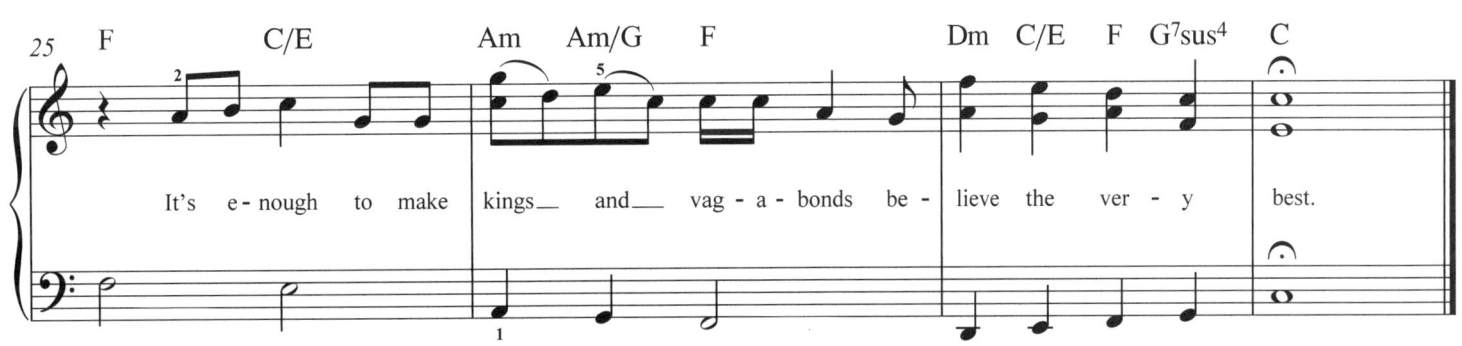

Goodbye Yellow Brick Road
Candle In The Wind
Words & Music by Elton John & Bernie Taupin

Candle in the Wind was originally released in 1973 having been written in honour of Marilyn Monroe. In 1997 Elton John did a remake of the song as a tribute to Diana, Princess of Wales. It sold over 600,000 copies on its first day of release and became the best-selling single of all time in the UK.

Hints & Tips: Don't be late with the left hand where it plays alone e.g. bars 7, 15 and 24. Also, try and work out where the beats fall in the syncopated bars. This will help you to understand the rhythm more clearly.

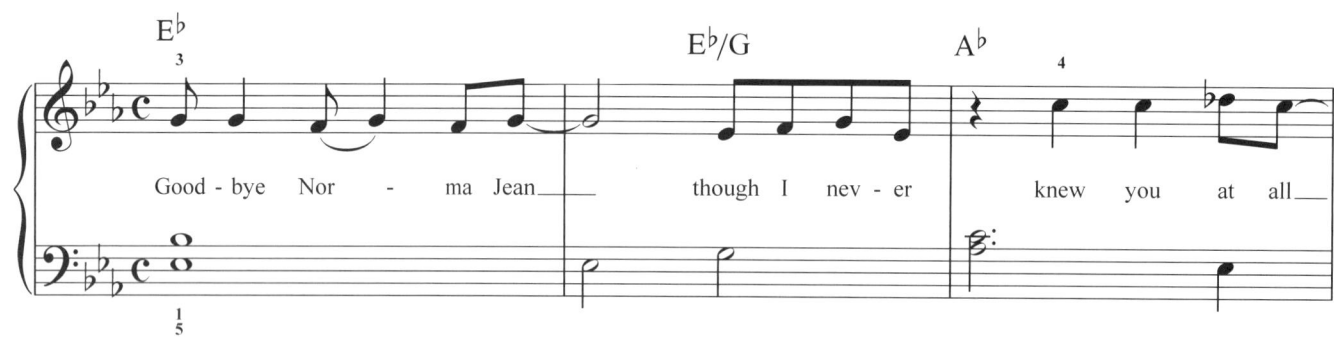

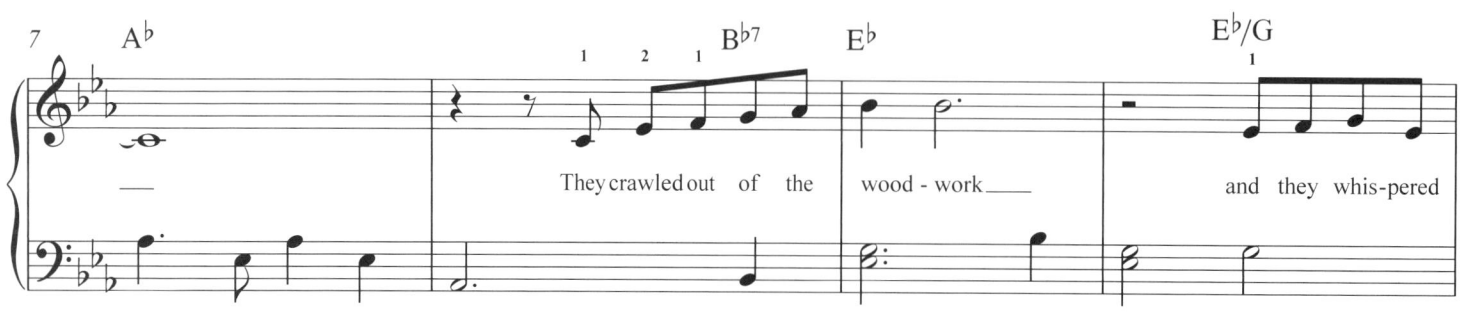

© Copyright 1973 Dick James Music Limited.
Universal/Dick James Music Limited.
All rights in Germany administered by Universal Music Publ. GmbH.
All Rights Reserved. International Copyright Secured.

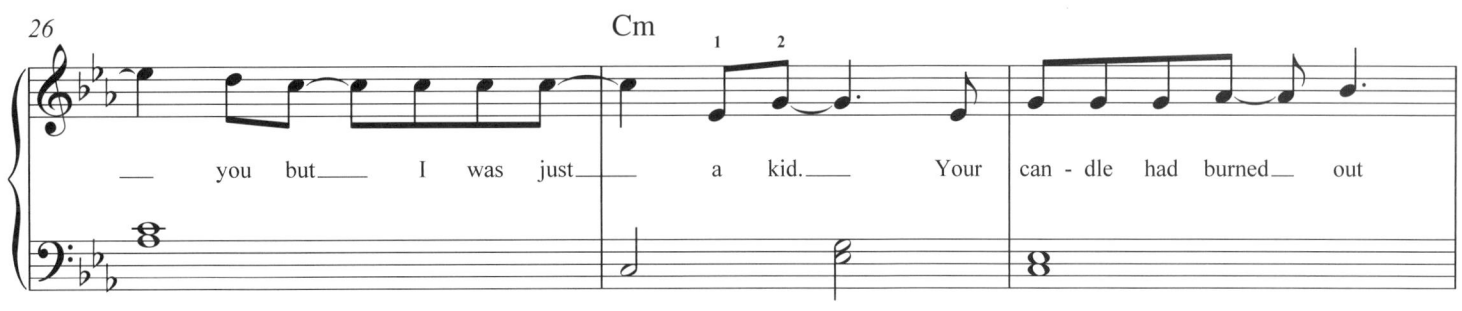
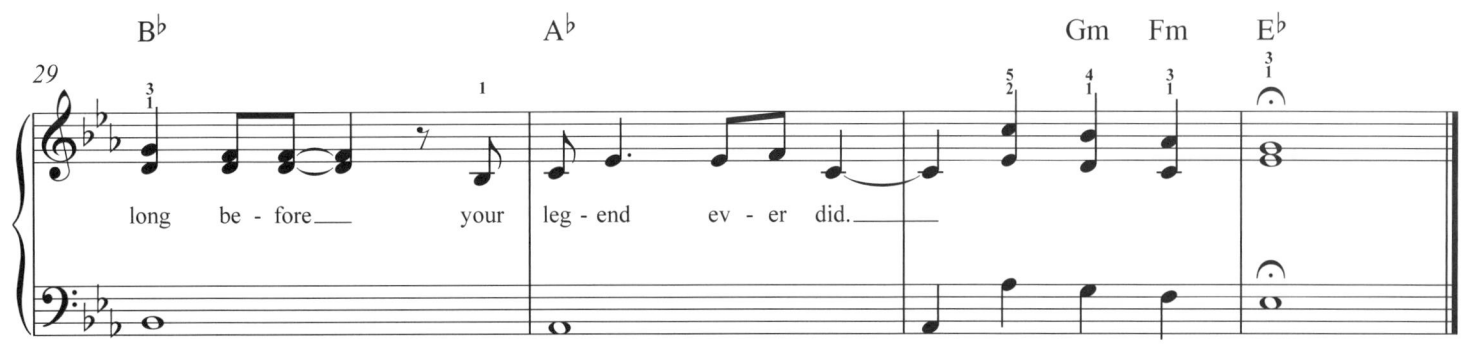

DON'T SHOOT ME I'M ONLY THE PIANO PLAYER
Crocodile Rock
Words & Music by Elton John & Bernie Taupin

Crocodile Rock, released in 1972, was Elton John's first US No. 1 single. The music is dominated by a Farfisa organ, instantly recognisable by its cheesy, carnival-like sound and honky-tonk rhythm. It was inspired by Australian band Daddy Cool and their hit single *Eagle Rock*, which Elton discovered during his 1972 tour to Australia.

Hints & Tips: Keep the left hand light throughout and use the repeated crotchets to drive the piece. Look carefully at the R.H. in bar 25 and the L.H in bars 29–30 so that the accidentals and fingerings don't catch you out.

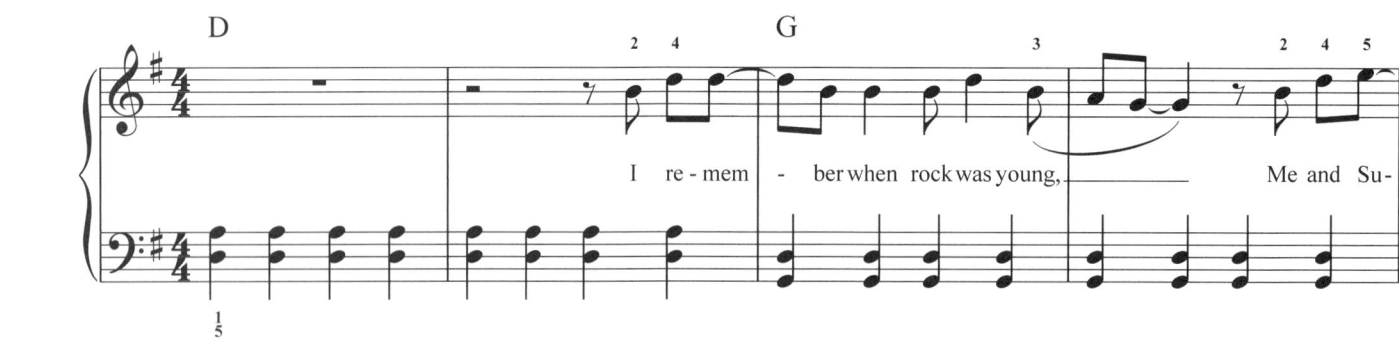

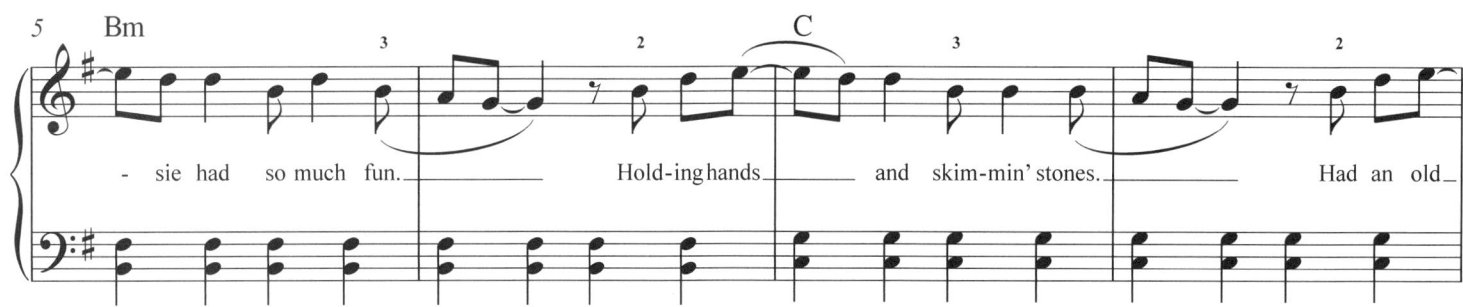

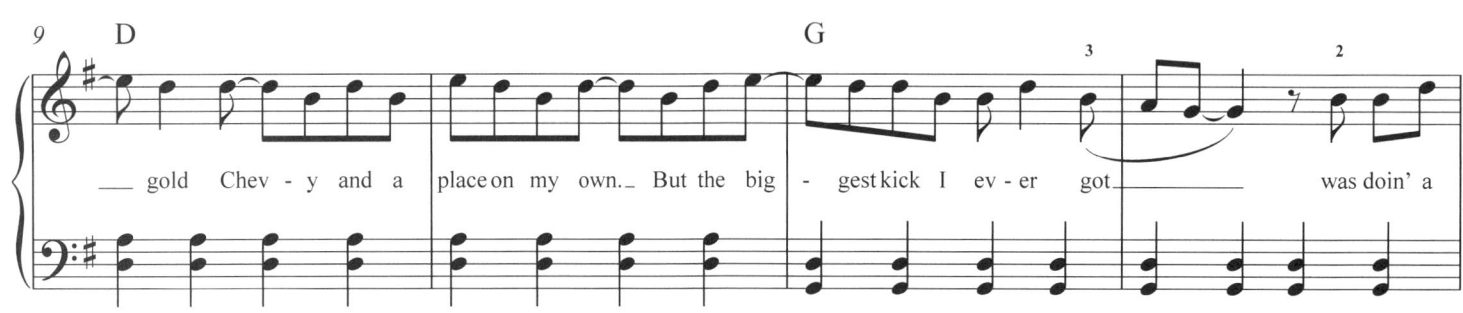

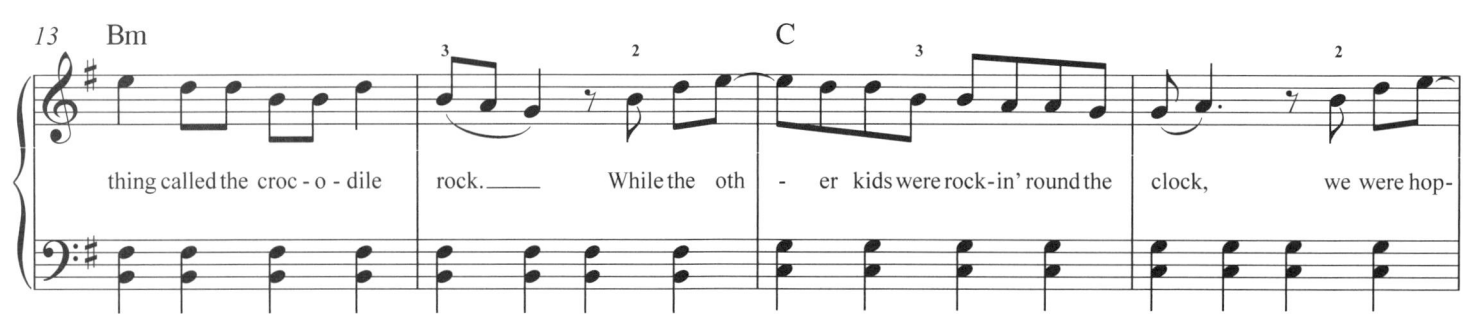

© Copyright 1972 Dick James Music Limited.
Universal/Dick James Music Limited.
All rights in Germany administered by Universal Music Publ. GmbH.
All Rights Reserved. International Copyright Secured.

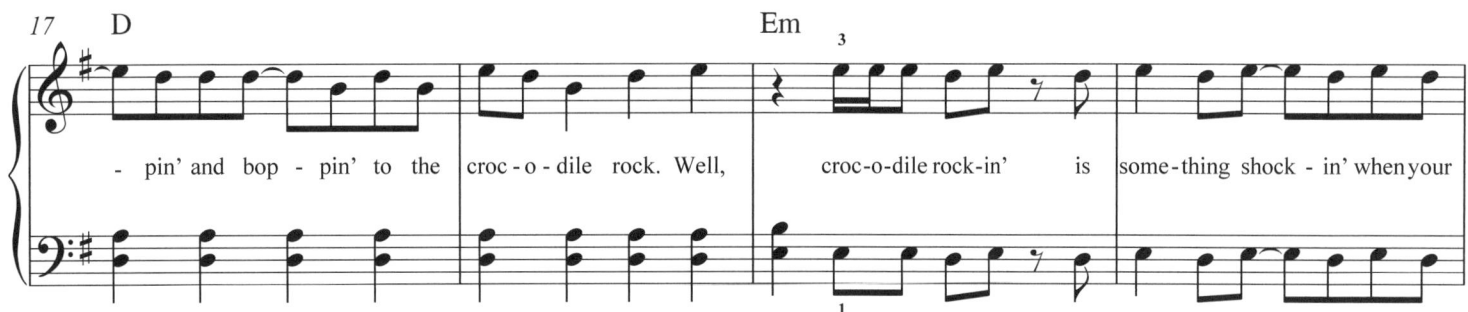
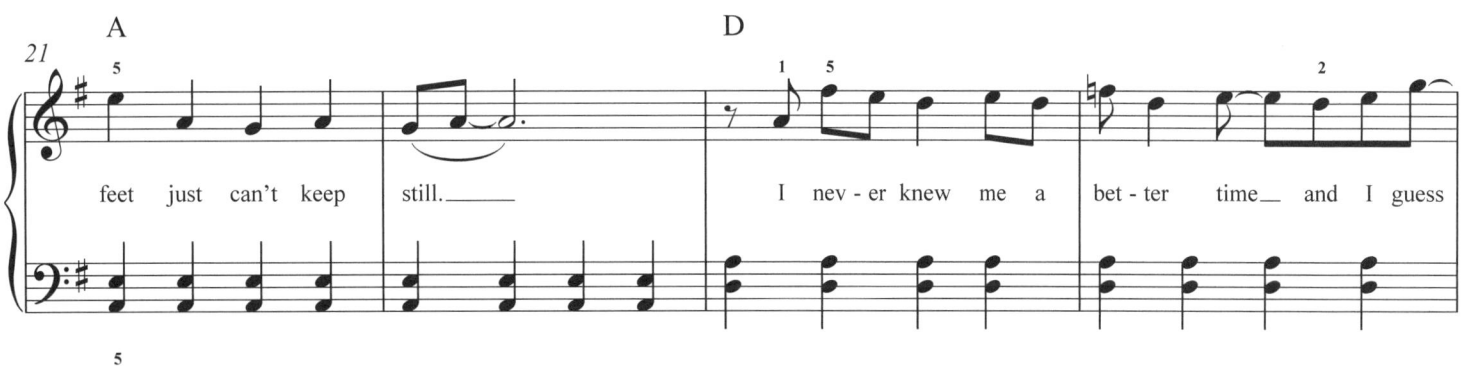
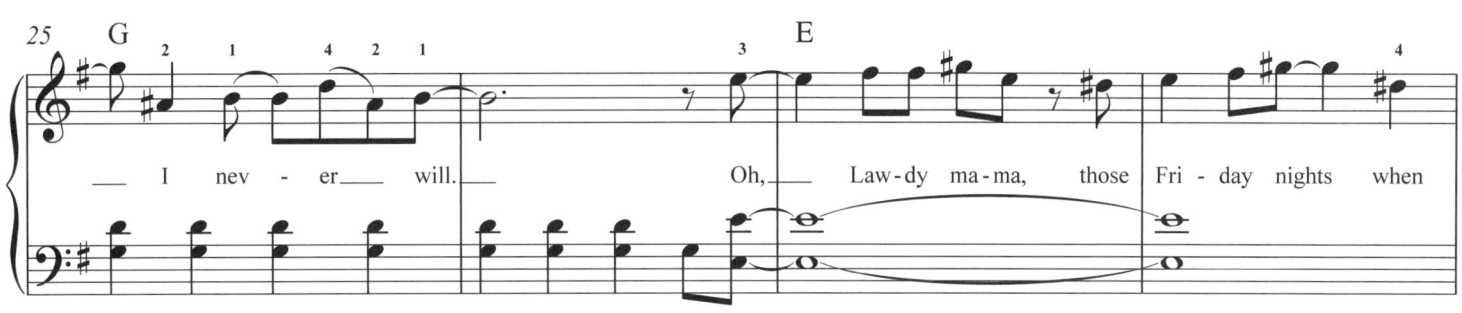
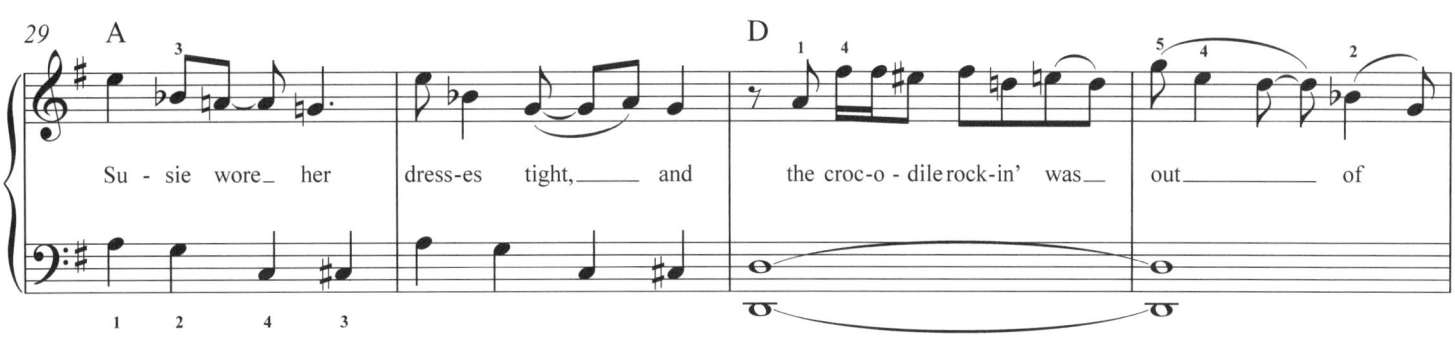
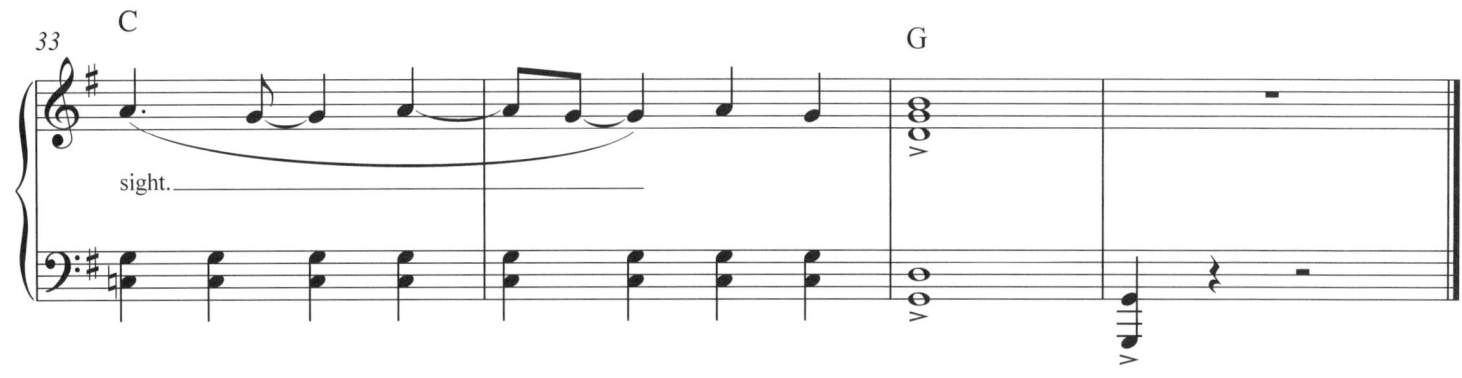

DUETS
Don't Go Breaking My Heart
Words by Carte Blanche. Music by Ann Orson

Don't Go Breaking My Heart was written by John and Taupin under the pseudonyms Carte Blanche and Ann Orson. A pastiche of the Tamla Motown style, it was performed as a duet with Kiki Dee and gave Elton his first UK No. 1.

Hints & Tips: The ascending scale in thirds (bar 18) is definitely the trickiest corner of this piece. Practise the right hand alone very slowly, starting by going up and down just a few steps, then adding an extra note at the top until you are playing the whole scale. Keep your wrist and fingers loose to avoid building up tension.

© Copyright 1974 Rouge Booze Incorporated/H.S.T. Management Limited.
Universal Music Publishing Limited.
All rights in Germany administered by Universal Music Publ. GmbH.
All Rights Reserved. International Copyright Secured.

CARIBOU
Don't Let The Sun Go Down On Me

Words & Music by Elton John & Bernie Taupin

Originally released in 1974, it was as a duet with George Michael, recorded live at Wembley Stadium in London on 25 March 1999, that *Don't Let The Sun Go Down On Me* had its greatest success. It topped the charts on both sides of the Atlantic and proceeds from the single were divided among ten different charities.

Hints & Tips: This piece looks harder than it is! Just take it slowly, pay attention to the recommended fingering and you will find that the notes fall comfortably under you fingers.

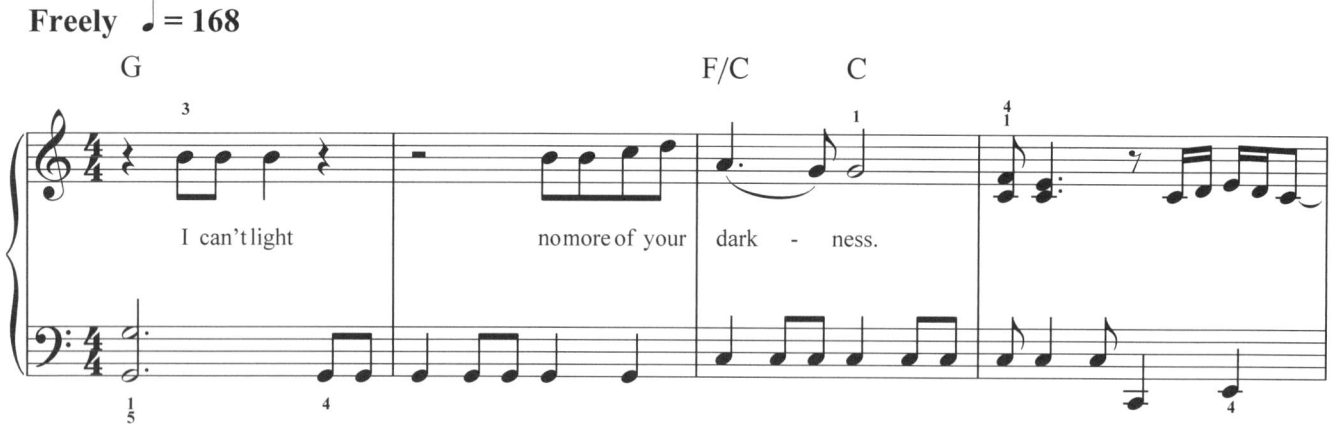

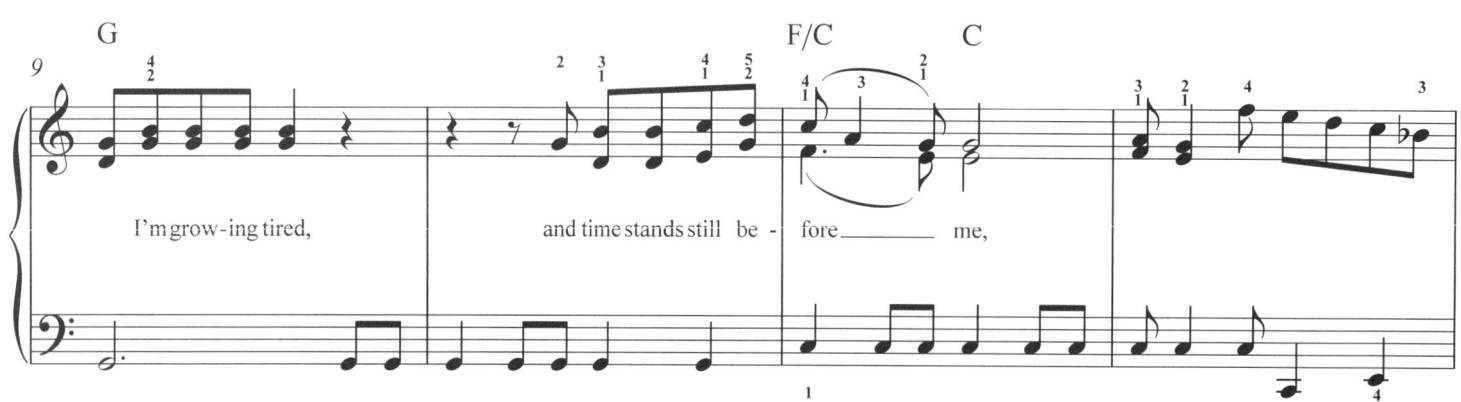

© Copyright 1974 Universal Music Publishing Limited.
All rights in Germany administered by Universal Music Publ. GmbH.
All Rights Reserved. International Copyright Secured.

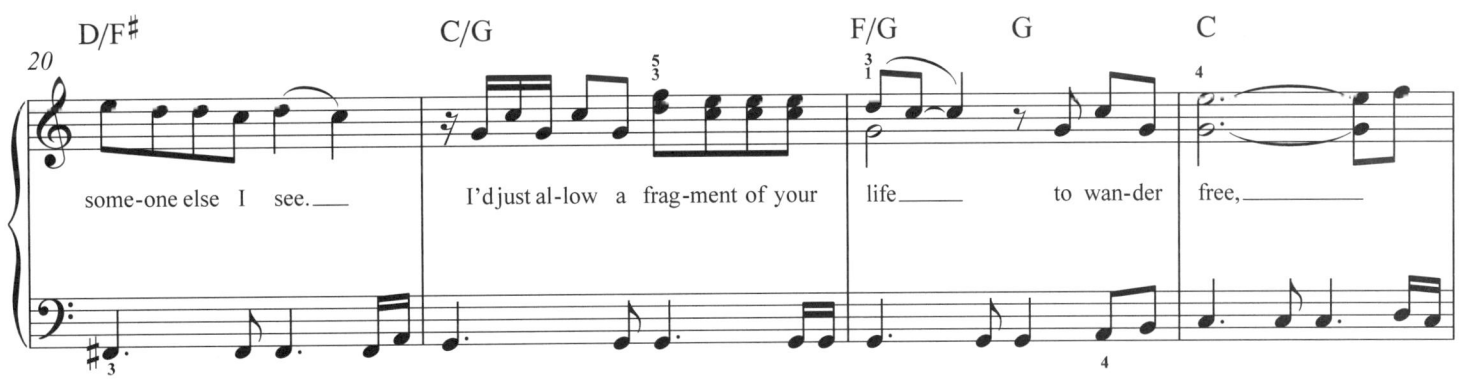

FROM 'BILLY ELLIOT THE MUSICAL'
Electricity
Words by Lee Hall. Music by Elton John

This song was written for the award-winning *Billy Elliot The Musical*, a stage production of the 2000 film. The book and lyrics were written by Lee Hall (who also wrote the film's screenplay) with the music composed by Elton John.

Hints & Tips: With three sharps in the key signature and a sprinkling of other accidentals in both hands you'll need to have your wits about you for the first nine bars. Try to look ahead as you're playing so they don't come as a surprise. After the key change it should be relatively plain sailing!

© Copyright 2005 WAB Management Limited.
Universal Music Publishing Limited.
All rights in Germany administered by Universal Music Publ. GmbH.
All Rights Reserved. International Copyright Secured.

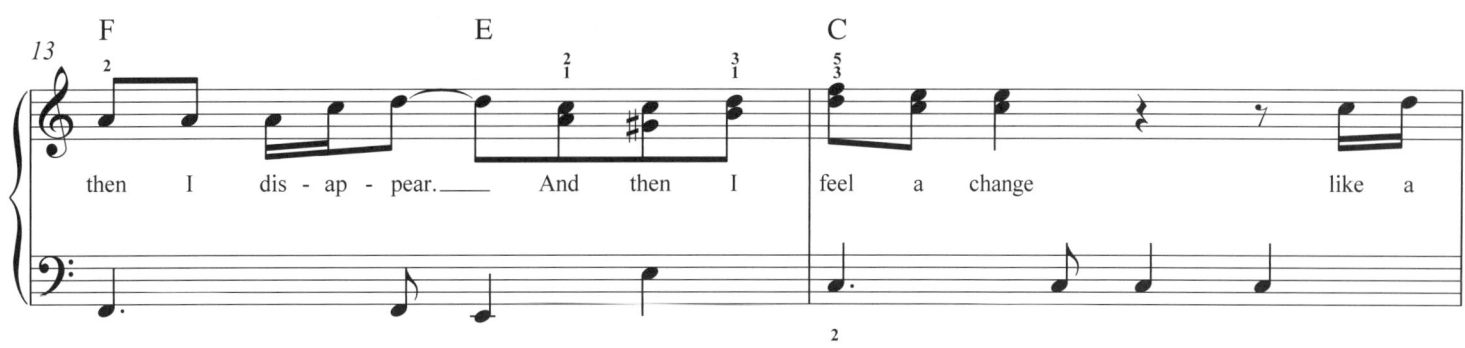
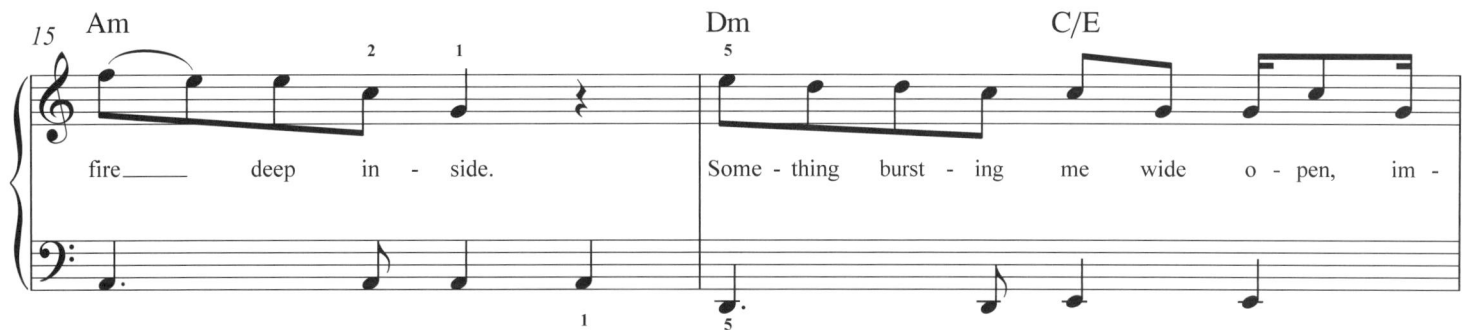
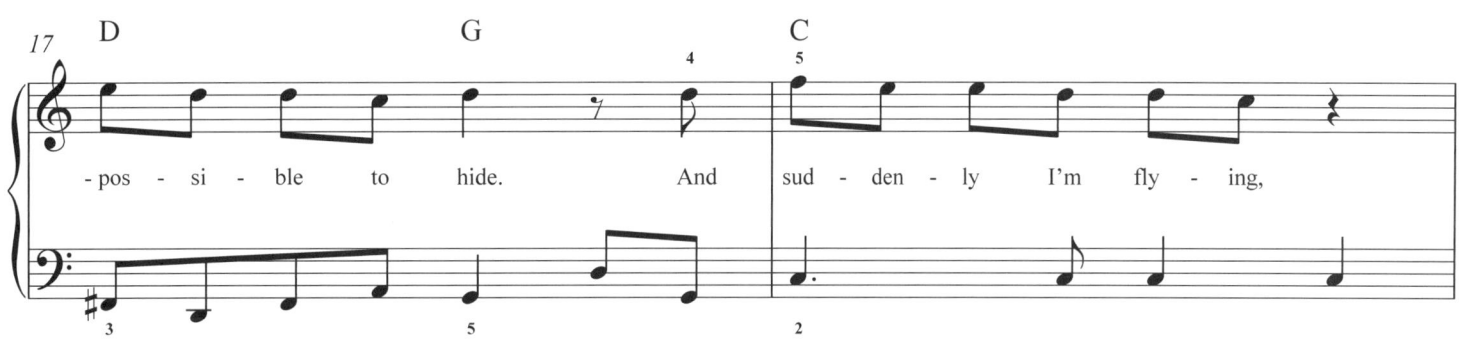
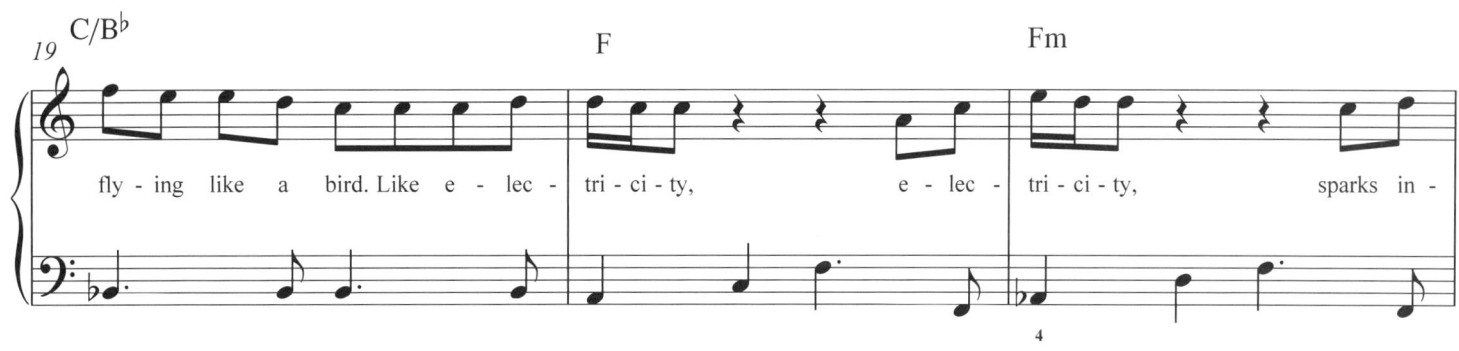

Goodbye Yellow Brick Road

Words & Music by Elton John & Bernie Taupin

This song tells the story of a young hopeful, his disenchantment with a promised land of opportunity, and their return home along the 'yellow brick road', imagery taken from the film *The Wizard Of Oz*. The album for which this single was the title track was ranked No. 91 on the The Rolling Stone Magazine's 500 Greatest Albums of All Time.

Hints & Tips: If you already know this song you will probably want to play it with a 'swung' feel whereby the first quaver in each pair is given greater length and weight than the second.

Too Low For Zero

I Guess That's Why They Call It The Blues

Words & Music by Elton John, Bernie Taupin & Davey Johnstone

I Guess That's Why They Call It The Blues saw Elton collaborate with yet another great musical artist by featuring the legendary Stevie Wonder on harmonica. It reached the Top 5 in both the UK and USA in 1983.

Hints & Tips: This song is in 12/8 which means there are four dotted crotchet beats to every bar, each containing three quavers. To help you place all the notes in the correct place, think about (and perhaps mark in) how many quavers make up the syncopated rhythms.

© Copyright 1983 Big Pig Music Limited.
Universal Music Publishing Limited.
All rights in Germany administered by Universal Music Publ. GmbH.
All Rights Reserved. International Copyright Secured.

SONGS FROM THE WEST COAST
I Want Love
Words & Music by Elton John & Bernie Taupin

Songs From The West Coast, the album from which this song was taken, marked a return of Elton to his piano-based roots. This song in particular was nominated for a Grammy, and the video featured actor Robert Downey Jr.

Hints & Tips: Don't rush through the semiquavers where they come at the end of a bar (e.g. bars 1 and 3). Instead keep a steady tempo throughout, perhaps using a metronome to help you, and think about the exact placing of the quavers to ensure accuracy in your performance.

© Copyright 2001 Universal Music Publishing Limited.
All rights in Germany administered by Universal Music Publ. GmbH.
All Rights Reserved. International Copyright Secured.

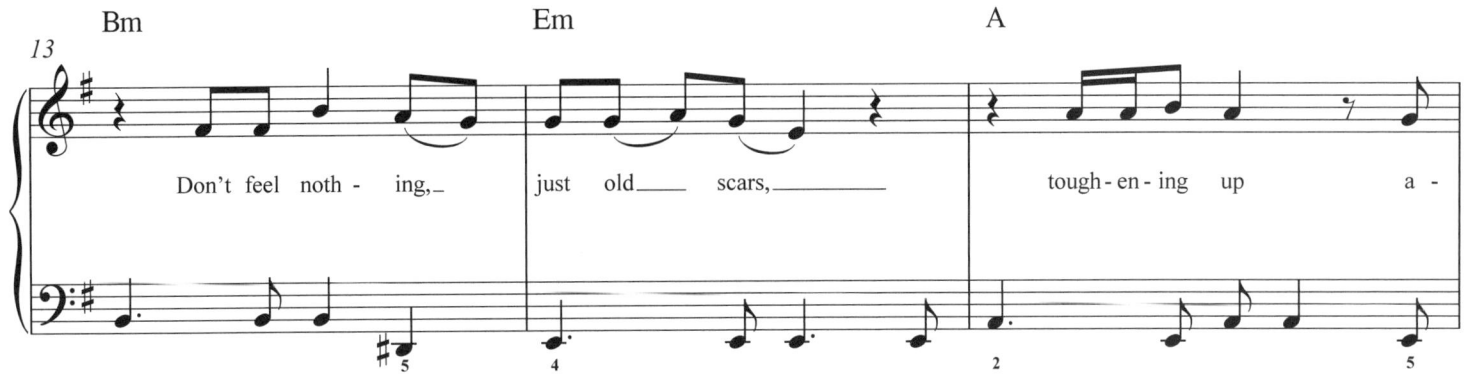

23

Too Low For Zero

I'm Still Standing

Words & Music by Elton John & Bernie Taupin

The first single to be taken from the 1983 album *Too Low For Zero*, *I'm Still Standing* was one of Elton's biggest hits reaching No. 4 on the UK Chart.

Hints & Tips: This is another 'swung' song (similar to *Goodbye Yellow Brick Road*) but it might be wise to practise it 'straight' until you are confident of where the two hands play together (e.g. bar 6) and where they are out of sync (e.g. bars 23–25) before adding in the swing!

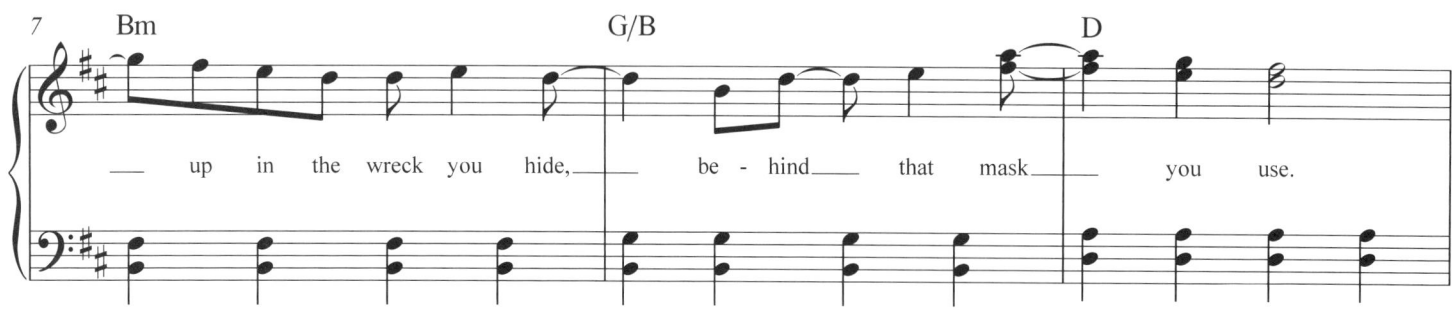

© Copyright 1983 Big Pig Music Limited.
Universal Music Publishing Limited.
All rights in Germany administered by Universal Music Publ. GmbH.
All Rights Reserved. International Copyright Secured.

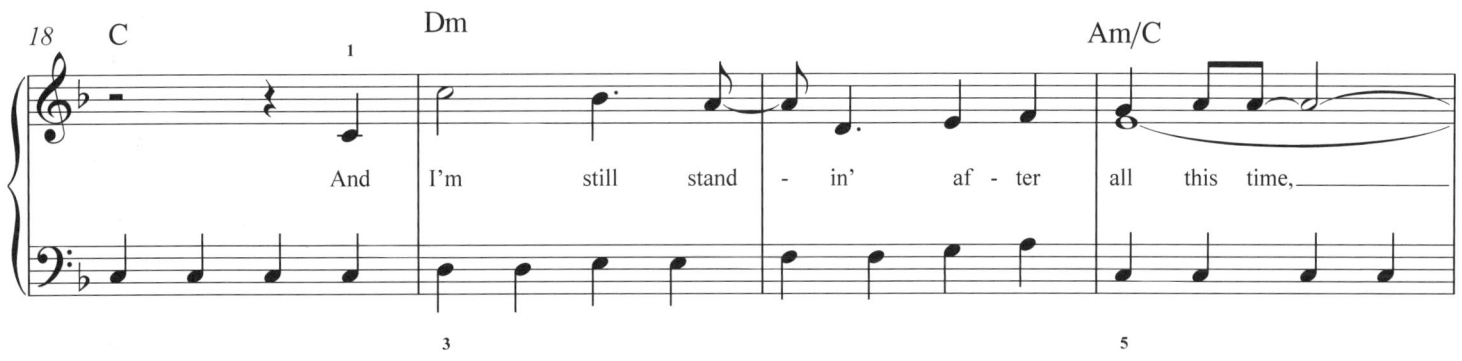

Nikita

Ice On Fire

Words & Music by Elton John & Bernie Taupin

Taken from his 1985 album, *Ice On Fire*, Elton wrote this song about the Cold War. In the lyrics he describes his crush on an East German citizen (Nikita) who he cannot meet because he is not allowed to cross the Berlin Wall.

Hints & Tips: There are a number of occasions in this piece where the last two beats of a phrase are not part of the melody (e.g. bars 2, 10, 12 etc). Instead they are a 'fill-in' between melodic lines. Some of them are a little tricky so isolate them, taking them out of context and practising them slowly.

© Copyright 1985 Big Pig Music Limited.
Universal Music Publishing Limited.
All rights in Germany administered by Universal Music Publ. GmbH.
All Rights Reserved. International Copyright Secured.

The One

Words & Music by Elton John & Bernie Taupin

The One is the title track of Elton John's 23rd studio album. Released in 1992, it was his first project since rehabilitation from drug and alcohol addictions, and bulimia. The album was dedicated to Vance Buck and features both Eric Clapton and David Gilmour.

Hints & Tips: To help you achieve a sense of line in this piece, look at two things: Firstly, if your hand cannot stretch to an octave, gently rock between the notes (bars 4 and 6). Secondly, work on the parallel sixths (bars 21 and 23) until you can play them 'legato' (smoothly).

© Copyright 1991 Universal Music Publishing Limited.
All rights in Germany administered by Universal Music Publ. GmbH.
All Rights Reserved. International Copyright Secured.

Breaking Hearts

Passengers

Words & Music by Elton John, Bernie Taupin, Davey Johnstone & Phineas McHize

Passengers was the second of four singles to be taken from the 1984 album *Breaking Hearts*. It reached No. 5 in the UK Charts but was not released as a single in America.

Hints & Tips: You will find your hands jumping around quite a lot in this piece. Look ahead as you play so you have time to prepare and move your hand to the correct position. Also, keep a loose wrist in bars 7–10 as this will help you play the triplets.

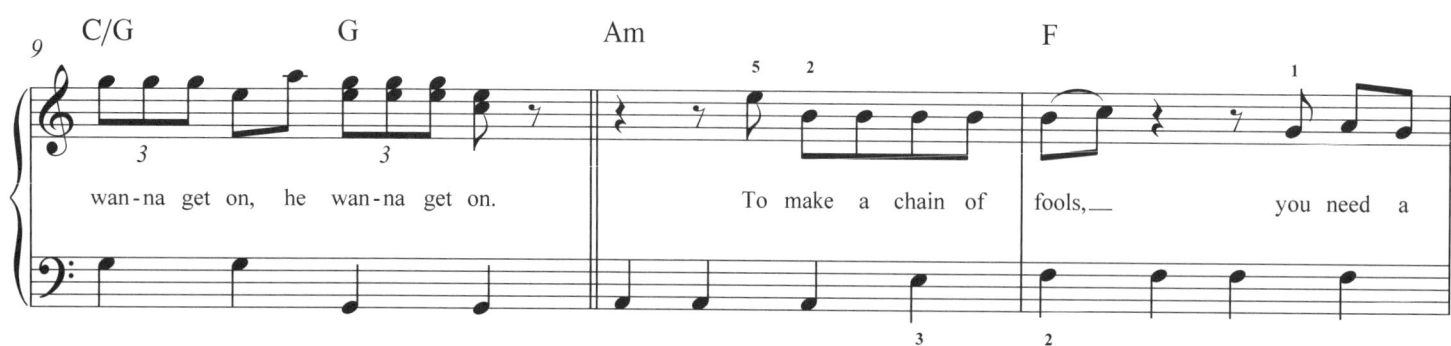

© Copyright 1984 Big Pig Music Limited.
Universal Music Publishing Limited (75%)/Warner/Chappell Music Limited (25%).
All rights in Germany administered by Universal Music Publ. GmbH.
All Rights Reserved. International Copyright Secured.

Honky Château
Rocket Man
Words & Music by Elton John & Bernie Taupin

At the time *Rocket Man* was written there was a great interest in space travel and, in particular, the Apollo 16 mission to the moon. The lyrics are based loosely on the 'Rocket Man' in Ray Bradbury's book *The Illustrated Man*.

Hints & Tips: This song has a complex and varied vocal line. The right hand imitates this, and if you find the rhythm tricky, try marking in the beats of each bar with a pencil. This should help you to fit the semiquaver rhythms with the left-hand part. The left hand stays quite still, so practise this first until it is secure.

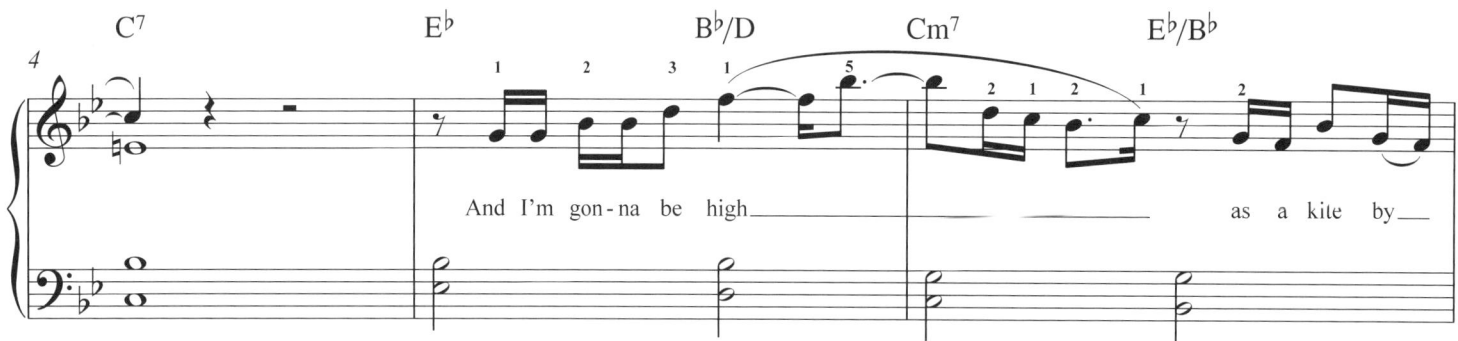

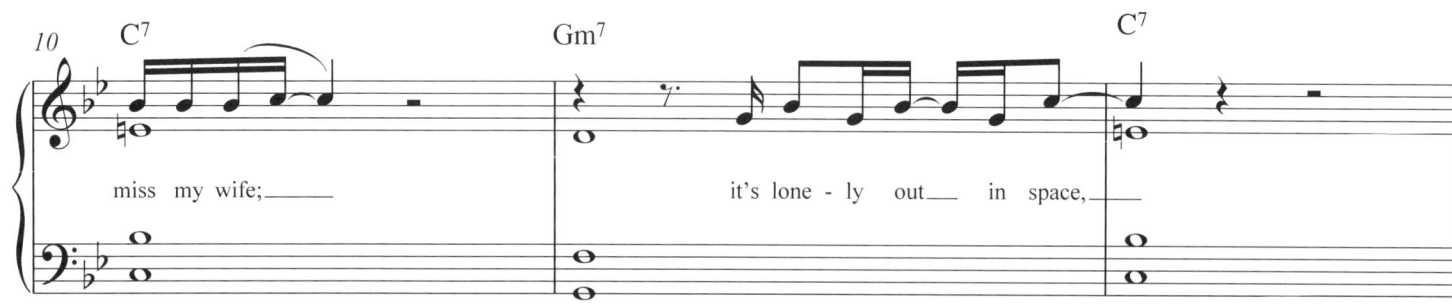

© Copyright 1972 Dick James Music Limited.
Universal/Dick James Music Limited.
All rights in Germany administered by Universal Music Publ. GmbH.
All Rights Reserved. International Copyright Secured.

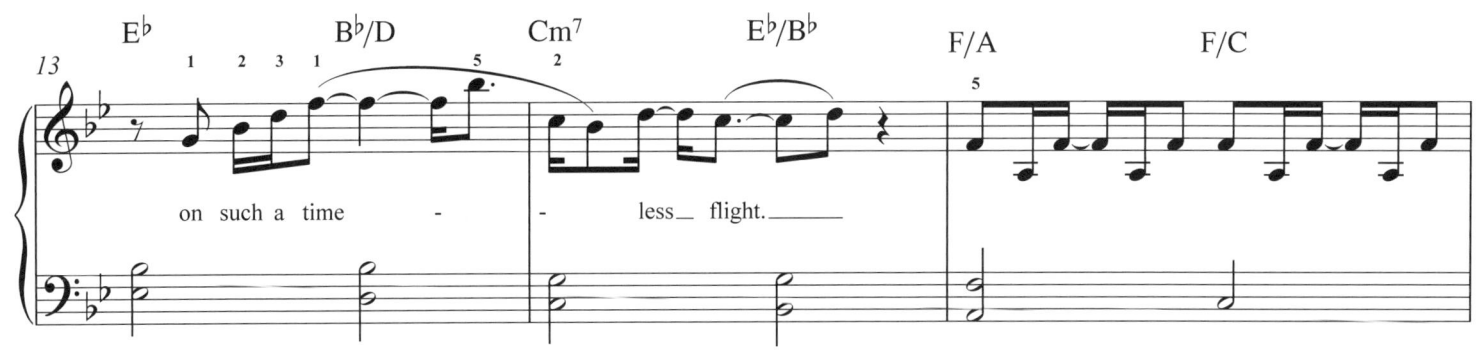

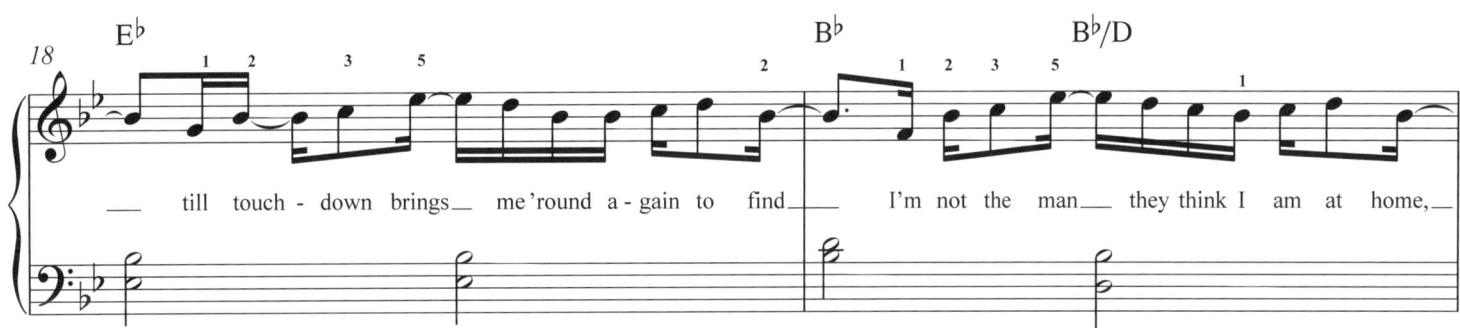
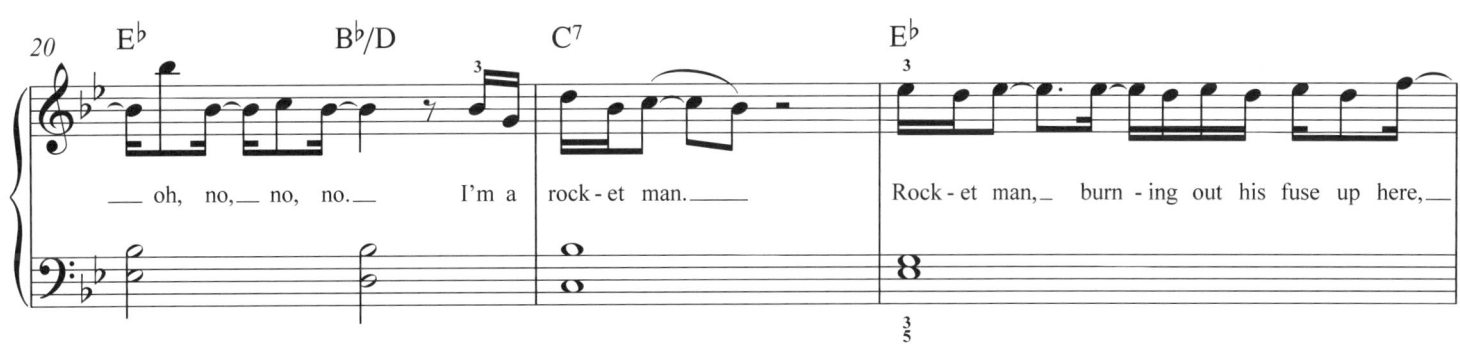

Sleeping With The Past
Sacrifice
Words & Music by Elton John & Bernie Taupin

Despite launching his career in the 1970s, *Sacrifice*, released in 1990, was Elton's first solo No. 1 on the UK singles chart. He had previously reached the top spot only once, duetting with Kiki Dee on *Don't Go Breaking My Heart* in 1976.

Hints & Tips: The interval in the left hand remains the same throughout this song so by keeping your hand in a similar shape, and moving it up and down the keyboard, your fingers should fall naturally over the correct notes.

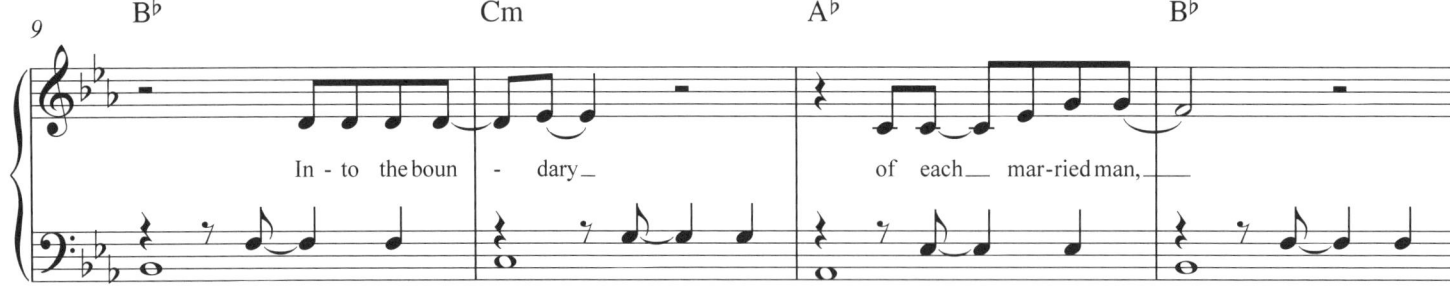

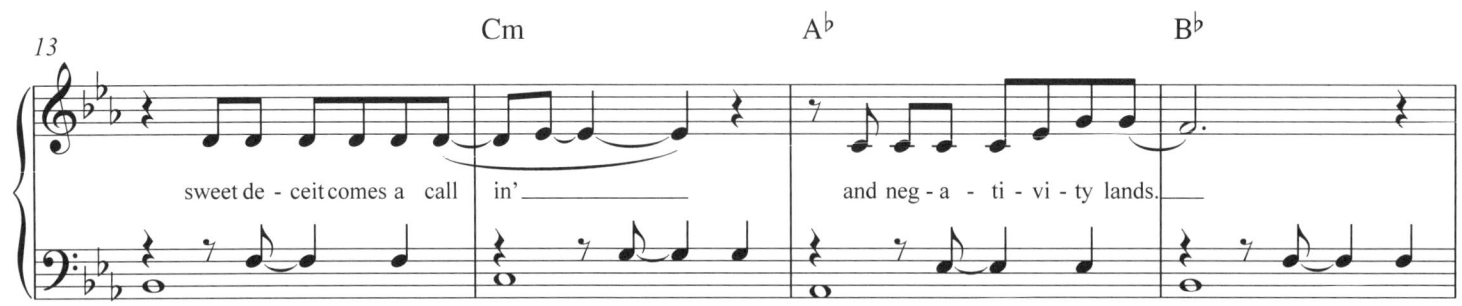

© Copyright 1989 Big Pig Music Limited.
Universal Music Publishing Limited.
All rights in Germany administered by Universal Music Publ. GmbH.
All Rights Reserved. International Copyright Secured.

Breaking Hearts

Sad Songs (Say So Much)

Words & Music by Elton John & Bernie Taupin

Yet another UK Top 10 hit for Elton, this song was taken from the 1984 album *Breaking Hearts* which featured the classic quartet of Elton John, Davey Johnstone (guitar), Dee Murray (bass) and Nigel Olsson (drums).

Hints & Tips: Practice this piece slowly, listening carefully, to ensure the two hands are fitting together precisely, before playing it at the tempo of the original.

Moderate Blues ♩ = 100

© Copyright 1984 Universal Music Publishing Limited.
All rights in Germany administered by Universal Music Publ. GmbH.
All Rights Reserved. International Copyright Secured.

37

GOODBYE YELLOW BRICK ROAD

Saturday Night's Alright For Fighting

Words & Music by Elton John & Bernie Taupin

Saturday Night's Alright For Fighting is one of Elton's harder-rocking songs, inspired by Taupin's raucous days as a teenager in Lincolnshire. It was the first single to be released from his seminal album *Goodbye Yellow Brick Road*.

Hints & Tips: Practise the right hand on its own to get your head around the many accidentals in this piece. Play along with a metronome to keep things in time and at a steady pace.

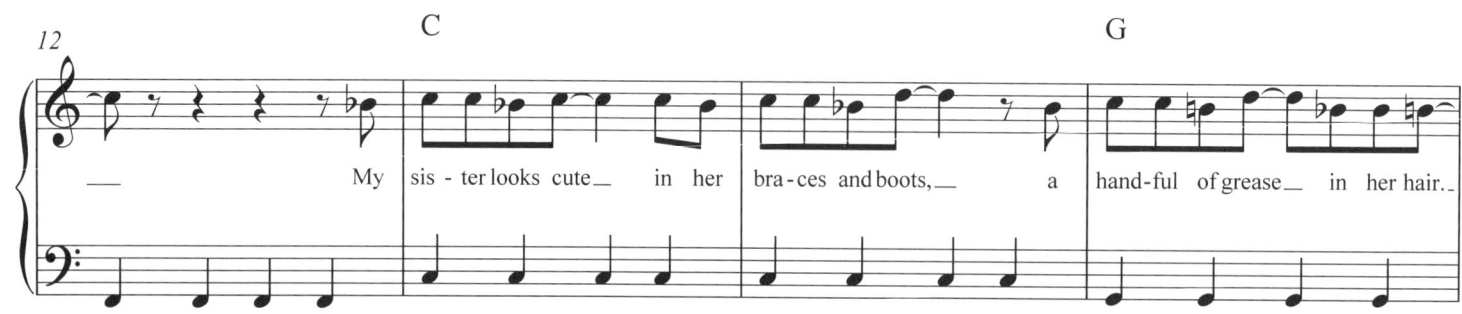

© Copyright 1973 Dick James Music Limited.
Universal/Dick James Music Limited.
All rights in Germany administered by Universal Music Publ. GmbH.
All Rights Reserved. International Copyright Secured.

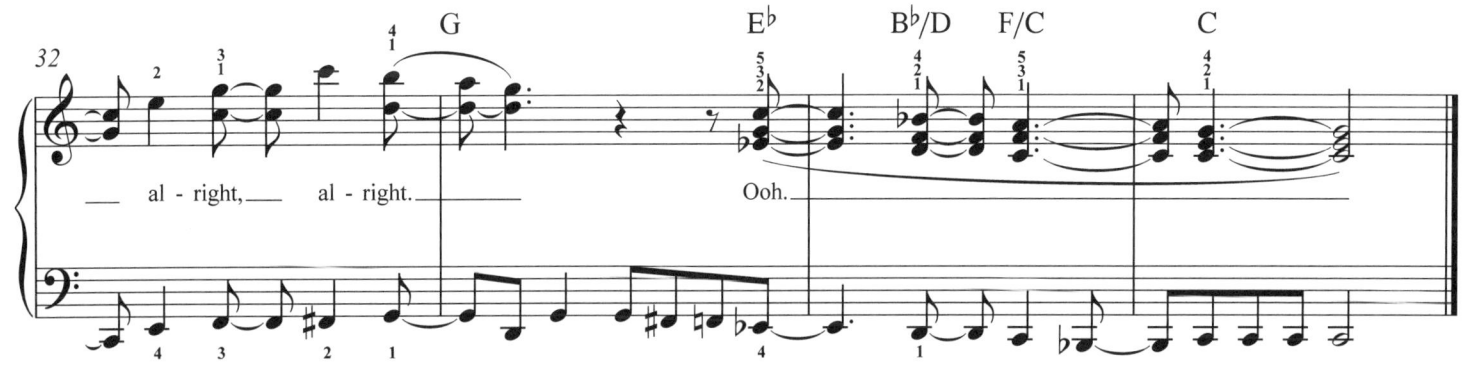

THE BIG PICTURE
Something About The Way You Look Tonight

Words & Music by Elton John & Bernie Taupin

This song was released as a double A-side single with *Candle In The Wind 1997*. It spent five weeks as the UK No. 1 song, making it the best-selling single ever in the history of the UK Chart.

Hints & Tips: Try clapping the syncopated rhythm found in the right hand in bar 3 before you play it on the piano. Note that the same rhythm appears again in bars 7, 11 and 15.

© Copyright 1997 Universal Music Publishing Limited.
All rights in Germany administered by Universal Music Publ. GmbH.
All Rights Reserved. International Copyright Secured.

Blue Moves

Sorry Seems To Be The Hardest Word

Words & Music by Elton John & Bernie Taupin

This is one of the few songs for which Elton wrote most of the lyrics as well as the melody. Whilst the original peaked at No. 11, a version of the song recorded with boy band Blue topped the UK charts in 2002.

Hints & Tips: Although on first glance there may appear to be a lot of notes on this page, a number of the passages are the same as others. For example, the first four bars of the left hand form a phrase that is played a further three times. Once you've cracked it the rest will come easily so it's well worth practicing.

© Copyright 1976 Big Pig Music Limited.
Universal Music Publishing Limited.
All rights in Germany administered by Universal Music Publ. GmbH.
All Rights Reserved. International Copyright Secured.

MADMAN ACROSS THE WATER
Tiny Dancer
Words & Music by Elton John & Bernie Taupin

Although Elton John didn't score any UK hits with songs from his fourth studio album, *Tiny Dancer*, written about Maxine Feibelmann, a dancer on Elton John's tour who later married (and then divorced) Bernie Taupin, remains a firm favourite among fans.

Hints & Tips: A number of the rhythmic and melodic patterns in this piece are repeated with different words. Identifying which phrases are similar and which are slightly different will help you master the piece more quickly so take a few moments to look through the piece with this in mind.

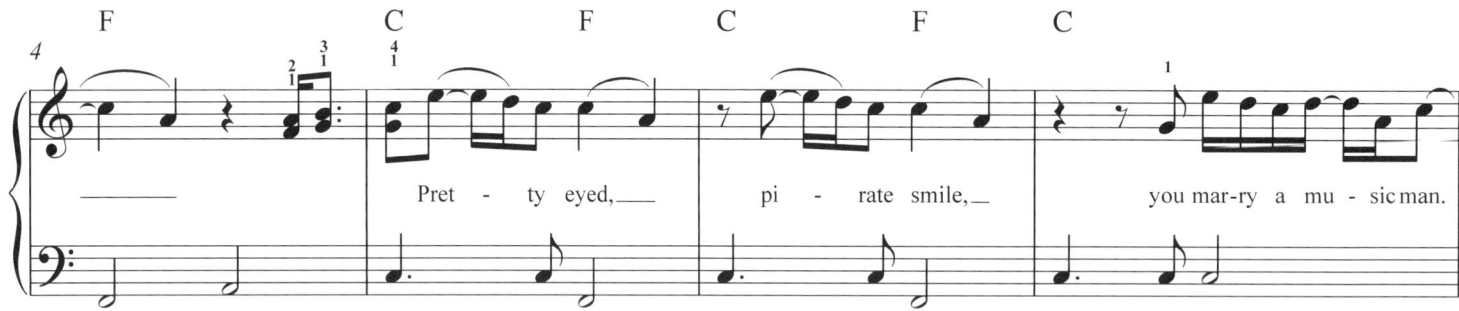
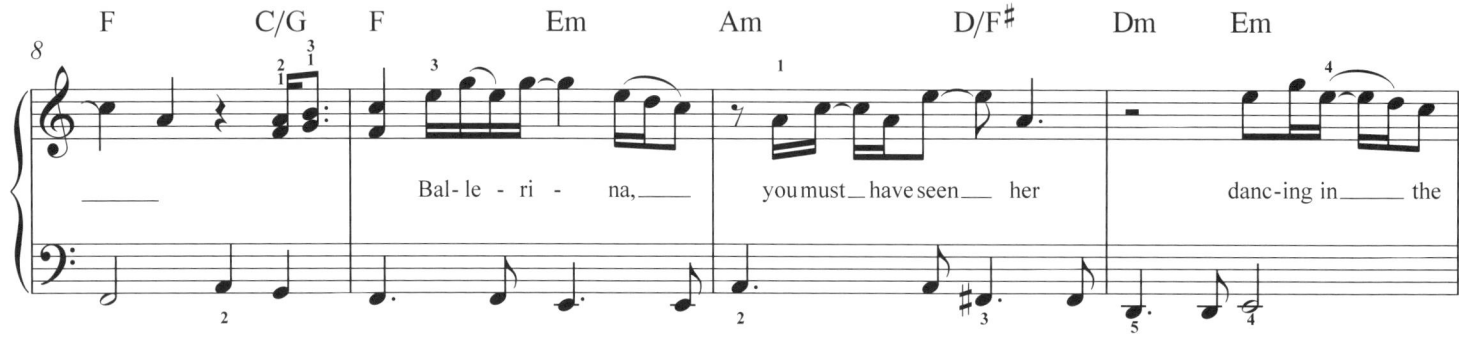

© Copyright 1971 Dick James Music Limited.
Universal/Dick James Music Limited.
All rights in Germany administered by Universal Music Publ. GmbH.
All Rights Reserved. International Copyright Secured.

ELTON JOHN
Your Song
Words & Music by Elton John & Bernie Taupin

Originally released in the USA as the B-side to *Take Me To The Pilot*, *Your Song* was preferred by DJs and eventually became the A-side. It went on to reach the Top 10 in both the UK and US giving Elton his breakthrough hit.

Hints & Tips: Try this piece hands separately at first as, once you have a solid left hand as a basis, it will be much easier to sit the right hand over the top. Take time to practise the first two bars slowly, gradually increasing the speed and eventually joining them onto the rest of the song.

Slow, but pushing forward ♩ = 60

Lyrics:
It's a little bit funny, this feeling inside,
I'm not one of those who can easily hide.
I don't have much money but, boy, if I did,

© Copyright 1969 Dick James Music Limited.
Universal/Dick James Music Limited.
All rights in Germany administered by Universal Music Publ. GmbH.
All Rights Reserved. International Copyright Secured.

46

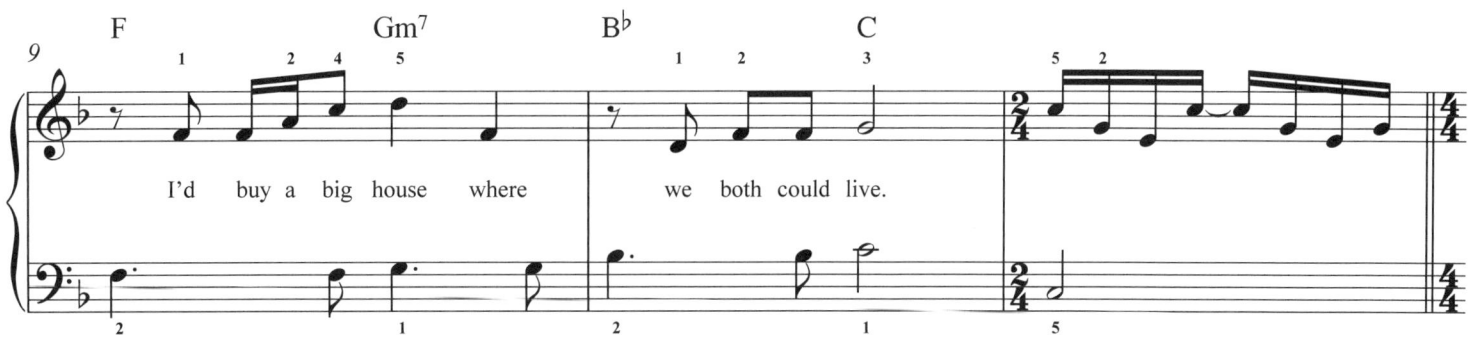
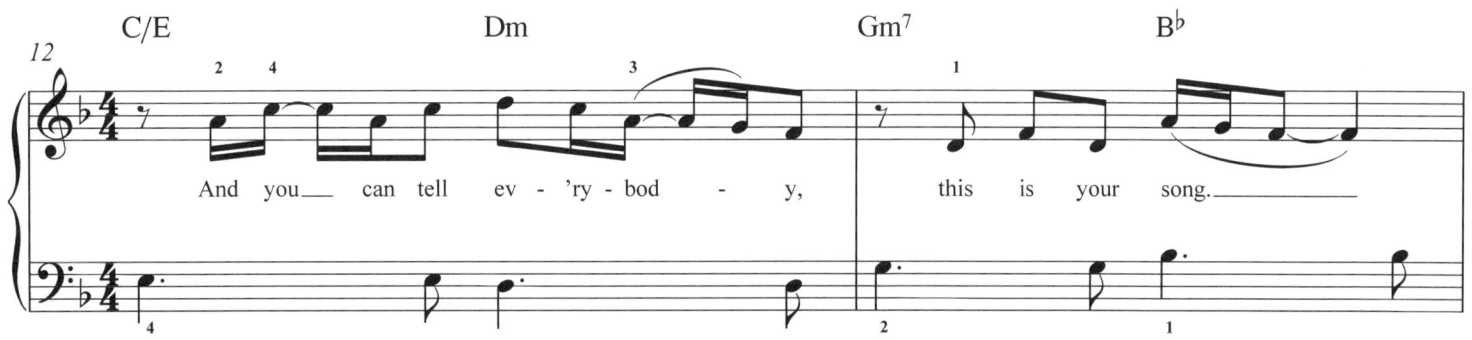
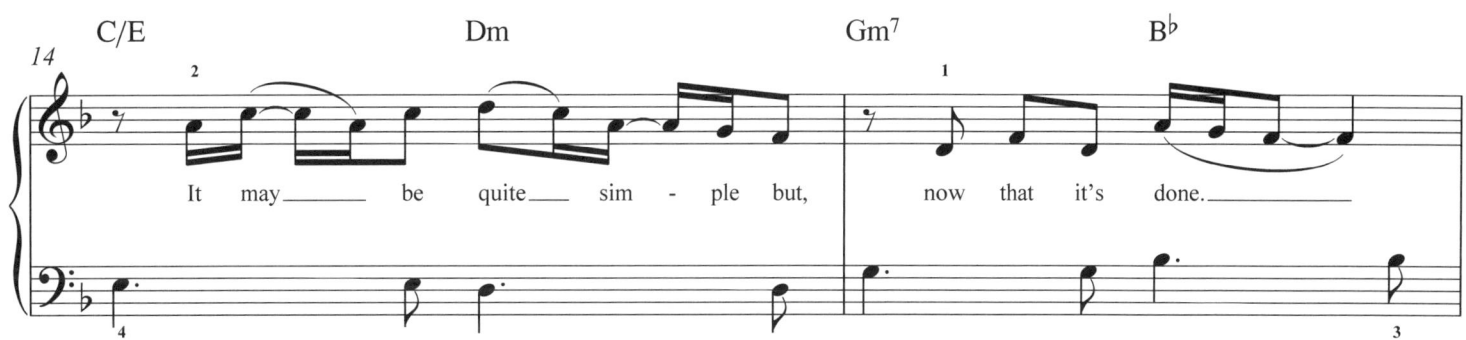

Don't Shoot Me I'm Only The Piano Player

Daniel

Words & Music by Elton John & Bernie Taupin

Daniel was inspired by the events of the Vietnam War. The lyrics describe a fictional veteran who was blinded as a result of the war, however, much of the meaning of the song was lost by the ommission of Taupin's final verse of lyrics when Elton wrote the music for the song.

Hints & Tips: When the right hand plays two or three notes at the same time (in bars 4, 12, 14 and 16), listen carefully to ensure that all the notes are sounding at exactly the same time. Practise them slowly if you need to.

© Copyright 1972 Dick James Music Limited.
Universal/Dick James Music Limited.
All rights in Germany administered by Universal Music Publ. GmbH.
All Rights Reserved. International Copyright Secured.